Bible Stories
GONE
EVEN MORE
CRAZY!

by Josh Edwards

Illustrated by
Emiliano Migliardo

CANDLE
BOOKS

Published by **Lion Hudson Limited**
Wilkinson House, Jordan Hill Business Park
Banbury Road, Oxford OX2 8DR, England
www.lionhudson.com

ISBN 978 1 78128 339 4

First edition 2018

A catalogue record for this book is available from the British Library

Printed and bound in China,
August 2018, LH54

Bible Stories Gone EVEN MORE Crazy!

Emiliano the artist has put EVEN MORE
funny mistakes into his drawings in this book.
See how many you can find on each page.

Use the Bible verses to look up each story
and help you answer some of the questions.

Can you spot the baby penguin in every picture?
Sometimes she appears more than once!

The Garden of Eden

In the beginning God created the earth.
He made the first man and woman, named Adam and Eve.
God gave them a beautiful garden to live in called the
Garden of Eden. There they spent their time happily
with all sorts of animals and birds.

Genesis 2:8–3:21

Do you know the name
of the big fruit tree?
(Genesis 2:17)

Which
creature is
wearing a
rubber ring?

How many
monkeys can
you find in
the garden?

Why does the snake wrapped around the tree have fruit in its mouth? (Genesis 3:1-5)

Can you find some animals playing cards?

Who named the creatures in the Garden of Eden? (Genesis 2:19)

Which animal is hanging out some washing?

Can you see the Loch Ness Monster?

Are there any unicorns in the picture?

Which creatures here don't exist on earth today?

Genesis 11:1-9

Why do you think everyone is arguing?

Why is this helmet the odd one out?

What are the builders driving?

Where did all the people go afterwards? (Genesis 11:9)

What has this bird stolen?

Can you see anyone drinking tea?

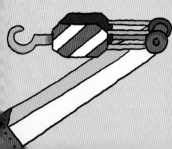

Where was this tower built? (Genesis 11:9)

The Tower of Babel

One day some men said, "Let's build a tower that's so tall it will reach heaven!"

They soon got to work and the tower grew and grew.

But one morning they woke up to find they were all speaking different languages. No one understood anyone else.

The tower never got finished, and it never reached heaven.

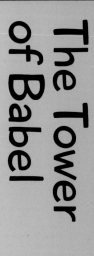

How many hammers can you find?

What has happened to this man?

How many levels have the builders made so far?

Do you know anyone who speaks another

The Golden Calf

Moses climbed a mountain. At the top he met with God. He was away so long that his people thought he had died. So they made a calf out of gold. Then they danced around it and bowed down to it.

At last Moses came down the mountain. He carried two stones with God's good rules on them. When he saw his people praying to the calf instead of to God, he was absolutely furious!

Exodus 31:18–32:19

Why has Moses smashed two stones?

Can you find a Spanish dancer?

Can you spot three people asleep?

Do you know the name of the mountain that Moses climbed? (Exodus 31:18)

What is this chef cooking?

Did people have phones in Moses's time?

What is this person putting in the pot?

How many different kinds of food can you find?

Whose idea was it to make the golden calf? (Exodus 32:2–4)

Why is this man knocking on the door?

Elijah and Baal's Prophets

King Ahab worshipped a god called Baal.
"Let's have a competition!" said Elijah. "We'll see whose god answers prayer." So they each piled up stones and put an ox on top. Baal's prophets prayed for fire: but there was no answer. Then Elijah prayed — and God sent fire from heaven.

1 Kings 18:38-39

 After three years without rain, what happened next? (1 Kings 18:41-46)

 What is Elijah holding?

 What is the man with the magnifying glass trying to do?

Who is the queen in the picture? (1 Kings 16:29–31)

How do we know the car has broken down?

What are they using to chop the wood for the altar?

How many prophets of Baal were there? (1 Kings 18:19)

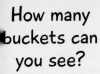 

How many buckets can you see?

Where has the queen left her crown?

Did they have fire engines in Bible times?

The Wise Men Visit Jesus

When Jesus was born, wise men saw a very special, bright star. They followed the star all the way to Bethlehem. There they found little Jesus with Mary and Joseph.
The wise men knelt before Jesus. They gave him rich presents: gold, frankincense, and myrrh.

Matthew 2:1–12

 What is chasing the mouse?

 Where is this soldier hiding?

 Where is the frog?

Who was the ruler when Jesus was born? (Matthew 2:1)

How many camels are there?

Can you see two women cleaning?

How did people journey in Bible times?

Can you find a selfie stick?

 Have the wise men brought the right number of presents?

 Is anyone missing from Jesus' family?

Zacchaeus

One day Jesus visited a town where a man called Zacchaeus lived. He collected tax money from people.

Zacchaeus was very small — but he badly wanted to see Jesus. So he climbed up a tree.

Jesus called out, "Come down, Zacchaeus. I'm coming to eat dinner with you!"

After he met Jesus, Zacchaeus was a changed man.

Luke 19:1–16

What do the film crew use this for?

Why is this man using a telescope?

Why do you think the people were excited to see Jesus?

Did people like Zacchaeus? (Luke 19:6–7)

Who is the dog following?

Have you seen anyone walk down a red carpet?

How many different instruments are being played?

After he met Jesus, what did Zacchaeus do with his money? (Luke 19:8)

What sort of tree did Zacchaeus climb? (Luke 19:4)

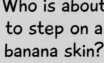

Who is about to step on a banana skin?

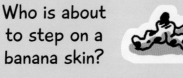

The Cleansing of the Temple

It was festival time. Jesus went to the Temple to pray.
But he found lots of people there, buying and selling.
"You're making God's Temple into a den of thieves!"
he shouted.
And he chased them all away.

Mark 11:15–17

Can you see any angry priests?

How many bulls are escaping?

Did they have a cash machine in the Temple?

Why was Jesus so angry?

What were the stallholders doing? (Mark 11:15)

Can you find a tortoise?

Who are the Temple guards running towards?

What is this man washing?

What does Jesus call the traders?

How many yellow birds are there?

Paul's Shipwreck

Roman soldiers arrested Paul because he followed Jesus.
They took him by boat to the city of Rome to be judged.
But a huge storm began and everyone was shipwrecked.
God made sure everyone on Paul's boat landed safely
on an island.

Acts 27

What is this
sailor trying
to do?

Can you
see anyone
surfing?

Can you
find a model
boat?

Why doesn't Paul look worried by the shipwreck? (Acts 27:24–25)

Did anyone die when this ship broke up? (Acts 27:42–44)

Which island did the survivors land on? (Acts 28:1)

How many Roman soldiers can you see?

Can you find the ship's anchor?

Have you ever been in a big storm?

What might be under the water here?

Did you find all the baby penguins?